Jackson Saves
the Moon

Words by Darren Garwood
Illustrations by Carl Osborne

Please scan here for the brilliant, "Jackson Saves the Moon Audio", read by Shaun Panda Nicolson.

SCAN ME

First published in 2020

Text copyright © 2020 Darren Garwood
Illustration copyright © 2020 Carl Osborne
Designed by White Magic Studios
ISBN: 978-1-5272-7249-1

I'm in my Pyjamas,
I've had my story read,
After a big kiss on the cheek,
I'm snuggled in bed.

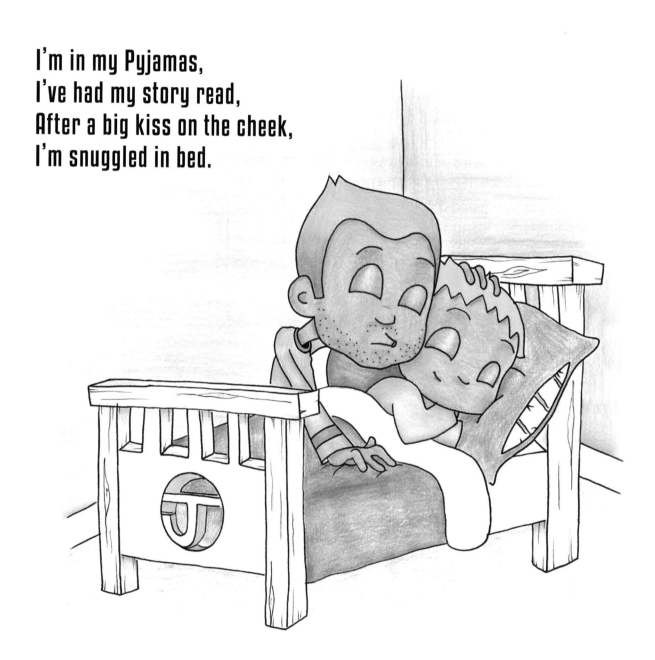

My eyes start to close,
but then I am awoken.
By beautiful bright stars,
and then these words are spoken.

"Quick! Follow us Jackson,
follow our shimmer!
The moon needs your help!
He's getting dimmer and dimmer."

7

So I follow their shine
whilst dodging space junk;
Hopping over a space camel,
diving under a space skunk.

Waving to the aliens,
(They live on Mars)
they have funny ears,
just like headlights on cars!

HEE HEE

Hello Moon,
you're looking ever so down,
You're normally so joyful,
I've never seen that frown...

With a tear in his eye,
The sad moon said,
"Well Jackson,
when I try to go brighter,
I get duller instead!"

The Martians lean in,
All together they say,
as their flickering ears
flicker away.

"Please come to a world,
where dreams are stored,
Let's have some fun,
so the moon can be cured!"

"Ok" I say -"let's get flying,
The Moon should be laughing,
he shouldn't be crying!!"

I'm sat on a rocket,
zooming deep into space,
I've never been this far,
I've never seen this place.

I'm in everyone's dreams,
Wow it's a world full of fun.
Oh no!! The fuel tanks are
empty!!
I fall fast onto my bum.

The first thing I see,
as the dust cloud settles,
Are clowns eating sandwiches,
lots of teapots and kettles!

I think as I've landed,
I've missed most of your spread,
Apart from the custard,
now over your head.

Oops!!!

In with my spoon,
oh, I just love eating custard!
"You're so silly," says a clown,
"I believe it is mustard"

My mouth is tingly,
and so are my toes,
I'm popping like crazy,
and I have a runny nose.

I start to hiccup,
my popping becomes loud,
the gas from my pops
forms its very own cloud!!

"Stop, Jackson, please,
I can't take this anymore!
I'm crying with laughter now,
I'm not sad like before."

"You being silly
And messing around,
helped me to smile
And to look up from the ground."

"The more the world laughs,
my shine becomes stronger,
So come along everyone,
let's laugh for longer and longer!"

NO chance

"I'm Earth's very own torch,
I'm powered by fun,
If the world laughs together,
I might outshine the sun!"

I'm now waking up,
Dad lifts me out of my bed,
I'm sure some mustard
just dripped from my head.

There's a letter in my pocket
It's from the aliens on Mars,
"hope you had fun tonight
with the clowns and the stars."

"If you're ever feeling sad,
look into the night sky,
If you search hard enough
you'll see the moon pass by,
If you then see a light flicker
just like on cars,
that's our ears flickering,
all the way from Mars."

Jackson Superhero might not be a real name, but it is a story about a real boy, and as the name suggests, Jackson is far from ordinary.

From birth, the real Jackson was like every other child. He passed all the regular milestones like talking, eating by himself and generally enjoying life. But just after his first birthday, Jackson started to lose key skills. This is when he was diagnosed with Krabbe disease and wasn't expected to live beyond the age of two.

By mustering all his strength, and with a lot of love from his mum and dad, Jackson is still doing well at age six. Jackson Saves the Moon was written by Jackson's dad. The moral of the story is that while Jackson's days may be limited, in the evening, when he dreams, he can be anything he wants to be.

We believe this fantastic story of a young boy going above and beyond will bring inspiration to parents and children who, for one reason or another, have to muster their superpowers on a daily basis. This book is for those who have to push back against daily challenges, for whom comfort and happiness requires extra patience, strength and love. Just as importantly, it's for those who rely on the support and inspiration of others. No matter what kind of day you are having, this book will still make you smile.

Printed in Poland
by Amazon Fulfillment
Poland Sp. z o.o., Wrocław